house beautiful

BEDROOMS

house beautiful

BEDROOMS

The Editors of House Beautiful Magazine

Louis Oliver Gropp, Editor in Chief ∽ Margaret Kennedy, Editor

Text by Cara Greenberg

HEARST BOOKS
NEW YORK

It is the policy of William Morrow and Company, Inc., and its imprints and affiliates, recognizing the importance of preserving what has been written, to print the books we publish on acid-free paper, and we exert our best efforts to that end.

Library of Congress Cataloging-in-Publication Data

House beautiful bedrooms / the editors of House beautiful magazine:
    Louis Oliver Gropp, editor in chief; Margaret Kennedy, editor: text by Cara Greenberg. —
1st U.S. ed.
              p.   cm. — (Great style series)
    ISBN 0-688-12587-5
     1. Bedrooms.   2. Interior decoration.   I. Gropp, Louis Oliver.
II. Kennedy, Margaret (Margaret S.)   III. Greenberg, Cara.
IV. House Beautiful. V. Series.
NK2117.B4H68   1996
747.7'7—dc20   95-38384
                                                 CIP

Printed in Italy
First Edition
1 2 3 4 5 6 7 8 9 10

Edited by LAURIE ORSECK ~ Designed by NANCY STEINY DESIGN
Produced by SMALLWOOD & STEWART, INC., NEW YORK

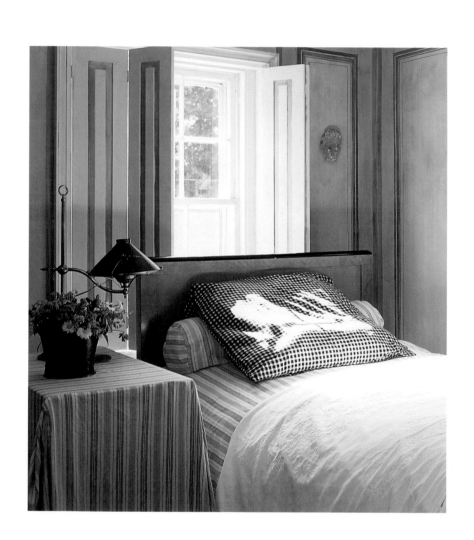

Contents

Foreword

The one exception to the generally simple, modern things in the Gropp household is our bed. It belonged to my wife's uncle; her father shipped it across the country to us after his brother's death. The bed is big and curvy, and it has dominated the decoration of our bedroom throughout our long married life. I'm not sure that I like it as a design, but I know it has played a central role in my family's life. I never feel more at home than I do when I climb into that tall, comfortable, and oh-so-safe piece of furniture. And I have wonderful memories of our two daughters, when they were much younger, clambering in to join us there on lazy Saturday mornings.

Let's face it: Bedrooms are important. The most personal and private of all the rooms in a house, they shelter us and our guests, provide comfort when we are sick or tired, and give us a space in which to enjoy our dreams.

Over the years we have found that readers always respond positively to *House Beautiful* issues that show a bed or a bedroom on the cover. Perhaps it is because these are the rooms we often wait to "do" after the more public rooms in our house are "done." That may be a mistake. *House Beautiful Bedrooms* was designed and written to help you correct that mistake as soon as you possibly can.

Louis Oliver Gropp
EDITOR IN CHIEF

house beautiful
BEDROOMS

Introduction

To the long list of things we take for granted these days, let us add the bedroom. It wasn't very long ago that separate chambers for sleeping were unheard of, and privacy for the individual was a completely foreign notion. In medieval Europe, whole families slept in the same hall-like room used for cooking, eating, and even sheltering animals. In the seventeenth and eighteenth centuries, to escape the hubbub in the main hall, some clever, well-to-do individuals conceived the idea of separate rooms for sleeping. By the mid-nineteenth century, bedrooms were commonplace throughout the Western world.

Yet in our fast-paced society, private time and space still seem elusive. The bedroom is more important than ever as a retreat, not just from the more public parts of the house, but from the chaotic world outside. With this primary purpose in mind, the decoration of a bedroom becomes a challenge of the most pleasant sort. The exact forms this may take vary widely ~ from lavish to spare, from traditional to idiosyncratic.

House Beautiful Bedrooms offers abundant proof that decorating the bedroom can inspire great flights of imagination. The boundaries of what is "permissible" have become wider and more expansive than ever, as we draw our inspiration from diverse cultures and the entire history of design.

On the pages that follow, you will find much of what you need to know to create the bedroom of your dreams. But we also hope you will enjoy simply perusing these beautiful rooms, and that you will begin to see their design possibilities in a new, more brilliant light.

Setting a Mood

n the geography of a house, the bedroom is the most private sanctuary, a place blessedly free from the public eye. The very appeal of a bedroom is that it is one's own, a place to go and close the door on the world. It is only natural that it is our most personal expression, the most self-indulgent of rooms.

Many people would say a bedroom should be restful, in keeping with its primary function, or perhaps romantic ~ billowing curtains, soft rugs, subtle lighting. But not everyone feels that way. "The bedroom should be as exciting and stimulating as any other room," says one designer, who uses lively colors, bold furnishings, and busy fabrics to implement her vision. "Cheerful by day, sultry by night," says a woman who, confined to her bedroom for months during a difficult pregnancy, chose a metallic wallpaper that metamorphoses by the hour with the changing light.

Whether the ultimate effect is clarity and calm, or a more energetic state of being; whether the desired feeling is historic or of the moment, sophisticated or rustic ~ the bedroom can truly be the stuff of dreams.

SERENE RETREAT

Two hundred years ago, a bedroom was called a cabinet, and it was often just that: an alcove in the wall, with panel doors that could be pulled shut for privacy.

"That's exactly what I wanted ~ a real get-away," says Spruce Roden, a New York City floral designer, of the master bedroom in his Connecticut country house, a central-chimney colonial dating from 1788. The decor was inspired even more specifically by a suite of Federal-period rooms at the Brooklyn Museum in New York City; Roden loved their clean lines, spare furnishings, and palette limited to just two colors. He captured that serene mood by designing a gleaming, snug, wood-sheathed box that gives its inhabitants the illusion of being totally removed from the workaday world.

The house, though old, was not historically important. "It had been messed up so many times, it gave me a certain freedom to mess it up my own way," Roden jokes. But he did make an effort to be true to the Federal period by restoring architectural details that had been stripped away during several zealous renovations. In the master bedroom, the walls were clad in raised pine paneling custom-made in the style of the eighteenth century, then painted a luscious blue-green. New closets, lined in cedar, are hidden behind doors covered with matching panels, which unify the room's perimeter and complete the effect of an

The lush romantic painting above the bed ~ a landscape coincidentally dated 1788, the same year the house was built ~ serves as decorative headboard and also keynote for the color of the walls, a true-to-period blue-green. Creamy linen sheets add to the restfulness and tranquility of the room.

19

enclosed "cabinet." Many of the furnishings and fabrics are true to the period, including a cherry four-poster bed.

Roden's masterstroke, lending distinction and a certain dressiness to the space, is the coffered ceiling, crafted by a local shipbuilder. The original beams, ravaged by age, were encased in pine boards, then painted glossy white. The result is a comforting space, far removed from the demands of the twentieth century.

Wool damask, the fabric of choice in fine Federal homes, is used for the sofa, draperies, and bedspread. An acorn-and-oak-leaf pattern echoes the acorn motif found on the four-poster's finials. The gold-trimmed sofa, a 1920s copy of a piece found in England's Knole castle, sits in front of a small French Directoire table. Both face a fireplace ~ a luxury on winter nights. The brass wall sconces are modern copies of a period design.

A ROOM WITH TWO VIEWS

The drama inherent in this Manhattan bedroom comes from the dynamic interplay of opposing energies. Owners Katie Ridder, a designer with a fondness for the decorative objects of the Middle East, and her husband, architect Peter Pennoyer, like things crisp and clean ~ and rich and sultry at the same time. The bed's white sheets, and the snappy blue and white striped curtains, for example, could belong to a beach house, while the richly colored folding screen and the arabesque-patterned wallpaper are evocative of a Turkish bazaar.

It is in fact the wallpaper that ties the room's two "personalities" together, literally reversing itself and transforming the mood of the room as the hours go by. By day, the walls are bright and reflective, making the room a cheerful afternoon retreat. Come nightfall, by the glow of brass table lamps, the metallic sheen of the paper tones down to matte, and the atmosphere becomes muted, romantic, mysterious.

At night, especially, the room seems removed from the city that surrounds it. "I love bedrooms that take you away from your environment a little bit," Pennoyer says. "The boring thing is to do a bedroom in a modern apartment pure and white." It is more interesting, he points out, to strike a completely different mood from the rooms you encounter on your way there.

The room's approach to color ~ a subtle handling of the three primaries ~ is a daring one. The warmth of the gold wallpaper makes the space seem to glow as if from within. The blue adds a complementary note of coolness. And touches of red in the fabric screen add interest to an otherwise nondescript corner. Ridder had originally chosen a complex-patterned fabric for the curtains, but Pennoyer vetoed it as "too expected." The couple opted instead for the lighter feeling of the blue and white stripe. The overall effect is energetic, eccentric, and offbeat ~ in a thoroughly comfortable, even luxurious, way.

Color, pattern, and time periods are mixed with assurance in this big-city bedroom. An eighteenth-century straight-legged side table in red maple and a brass lamp by early modernist designer

Walter von Nessen share a cozy corner. The headboard and bedskirt sport the same summery blue and white fabric as the curtains. Simple sisal carpeting quietly pulls the room together.

A screen made from fabric from a 1920s theater set incorporates the three primary colors that dominate the room's palette (near right). Amid the exuberant pairing of pattern and color in their master bedroom, white bed linens and a white-draped nighttable provide a few oases of calm (far right). A yellow slipcovered vanity chair keeps company with a birch Biedermeier-style dressing table, crafted in Scandinavia in the 1870s (below right).

AUSTERE BEAUTY WITH A PAST

It takes a reverence for the past to appreciate the gentle, evocative beauty of the rather spare guest bedroom in this 1762 clapboard relic of colonial New England. Here, the mood is one of deep repose. "We wanted to keep it tranquil and calm and authentically of the period," says one of the owners. "Nothing glitzy or jarring that would make someone say, 'Yes, they must have redone this place in the late eighties.'"

Carefully edited and composed by master designer John Saladino, the room is as dignified and pure, and as starkly dramatic, as a Quaker meetinghouse. Yet it also radiates great warmth. "I wanted it to glow at night like the inside of an old lantern," says Saladino. And so it does: The desired rich tallow color was achieved in a two-step process. First, solid ochre paint was applied to the walls as a ground. Then, in a paint technique known as sponge-glazing, a warm cognac color was layered over it.

In fact, the walls in the guest bedroom were the only surfaces that were painted. The original paneled door and window moldings were dry-scraped and intentionally left in rough condition. That approach coincided with the owners' treatment of the entire house, which had never been modernized. Over the generations, numerous coats of paint and wallpaper had virtually encrusted every room. Most surfaces were simply hand-stripped, then left alone, resulting in the mottled, corroded look of broken walls unearthed at an archaeological site.

A pair of reproduction Shaker-style cherry wood beds, their canopies undraped, are compatible with the pristine starkness of the space ~ a starkness relieved only by a pair of white heirloom candlewick coverlets crocheted by the grandmother of one of the owners.

The conscious restraint shown in furnishing the room is in deference to the house's age. Citing details such as the original wide panel doors, the elliptical arch of the fireplace, the wonderful patina of the window casing, and the old glass in the panes, Saladino says, "If we had overfurnished it, some of those subtleties would have been lost."

Even without a blaze, the pure lines of the guest bedroom's big working fireplace are a strong focal point in this New England landmark remodeled by John Saladino. Flanking the hearth are a Mission-style oak chair by Stickley Brothers and a genuine Shaker rocker bought at auction. The kilim rug brings out the cinnamon color of the walls.

There was no need
to fake age in this house.
An appreciation of
its effects is evident in
the treatment ~ or rather
nontreatment ~ of the
scratched and worn
bedroom door, moldings,
and trim (above left), as
well as the window
moldings left unrestored
and bare (below left).
Crocheted bed coverlets
paired with heavy
khaki and cream-striped
canvas spreads and
a geometric-pattern rug
provide softness in
an otherwise austere
room (opposite).

GILDED SIMPLICITY

O nly a very skillful mood-maker like Charles Spada could take two very different qualities ~ guilelessness and sophistication ~ and play them against each other so as to bring out the best in each. "I love incongruous things together," says the Boston-based interior designer. This Connecticut stone house, built a century ago by a Tuscan immigrant and refurbished by Spada, retains all the unpretentious roughness of an old-world dwelling. Yet its furnishings, mostly European antiques of good pedigree, reveal the cultivated tastes of an esthete.

In the renovation of the second-story bedroom, as in the rest of the once-disastrous interiors, Spada encouraged the rustic nature of the house, built from local stone and hand-mixed sand mortar, to shine through. The designer deliberately left the floors bare, bypassed wallpaper and printed fabrics, and used only white paint on walls restuccoed in the crude European manner.

The bedroom's original low pine ceilings (only 6 feet 8 inches high) and wide-board wood floors form an envelope for outstanding antiques. The highly polished woods of the eighteenth-century pieces and a gilded Italian mirror are lustrous against the matte finish of the stucco walls. The overall effect is intentionally spare. "When a room is terribly filled with color and objects," says Spada, "you can't concentrate on anything."

Deep-set casement windows reveal the sturdy construction of this old New England house. Shown off against the original wood ceiling and old wood floors of the master bedroom, fine antiques ~ a gilded Italian mirror, Swedish grain-painted writing table, cane-back French chair, and English bench set at the foot of the bed ~ add notes of sophistication and polish.

An early-nineteenth-
century tea table
of English oak and a
headboard of inlaid
Italian fruitwood are
typical of the carefully
chosen antiques that
elevate the room above
its simple architecture
(above). A lush Italian
painting of the late
nineteenth century echoes
the room's neutral
palette (right). There are
no bureaus or chests of
drawers in this room; a
new bank of closets
and bookshelves, built
in along one wall, fills
all storage needs.
The room's eclectic fur-
nishings include a Syrian
traveling chest inlaid
with mother-of-pearl and
ebonized and gilded
Italian wall sconces
(opposite).

CHAPTER **2**

Questions of Balance

he most successful decorating is often a delicate balancing act, a tightrope walk between playing it too safe and going over the top. A bedroom that is "all one thing" ~ religiously of a single style or period, say, or burdened with an overabundance of pattern, or spare without relief ~ can quickly become tiresome.

Dynamism comes from the conjunction of opposing elements, whether in terms of texture (the roughness of a sisal rug against the sheen of highly polished woods, for example), color (a jolt of bright red against a pale background), or attitude (a seashell on a fine antique piece).

Always, balance and harmony imply careful editing of furnishings and accessories. Sometimes, says designer De Bare Saunders, being out of scale is more interesting than being in scale. "Rules are for students," he says. For John Saladino, there is one abiding principle: "Things that go into a room must have respect for one another, even though those objects may be of totally opposite character. People who just jam everything into a beautiful room risk losing its proportions."

COOL AND CLASSIC

In the manner of his mentor, master decorator Billy Baldwin, Frank Babb Randolph often works with traditional elements ~ French furniture, fine antiques ~ and his approach often incorporates Baldwin principles such as using inexpensive fabrics on costly pieces of furniture. But the crisp lines of the bedrooms in his own home reveal the soul of a modernist.

Equilibrium in his Washington, D.C., bedroom begins with the bed itself: Centered in the room, it seems to float from the ceiling with the grace of a trapeze. The simple canopy, made from lengths of white cotton suspended from a thin wood frame, is open and airy, yet offers a sense of cozy enclosure. Although the room has 8-foot ceilings, "you feel you've entered a very grand room at least 10 feet tall," says Randolph.

The guest bedroom is as refined and carefully edited as the master bedroom ~ a kind of cool, clean extension of it, with snowy walls and tab curtains of the same burlap-textured linen. In both rooms, found objects such as shells picked up on the beach are mixed with expensive antique furnishings in yet another striking juxtaposition. "These are the things we see in nature," says the designer. "Why shouldn't we live with them?"

In each room, furniture stands out in silhouette against the white walls and woodwork. A quiet backdrop, says Randolph, "makes furniture legs seem to dance."

In the master bedroom (opposite), light floods in through new clean-lined French doors hung with tab curtains of hand-woven Nantucket linen. A fine eighteenth-century chair wears natural-colored woven linen (above); designer Frank Babb Randolph's childhood teddy bear keeps things from becoming too serious.

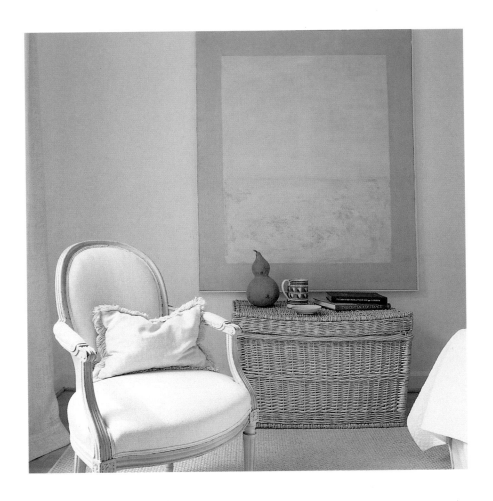

The designer's democratic approach to decorating is evident in almost every corner, where fine antiques mingle with humbler pieces. In the guest room (above), where a large abstract painting sets the stage for a harmonious scheme of neutrals, an inexpensive wicker trunk for storing extra blankets hobnobs with a serious French antique chair.

Propped on the room's eighteenth-century Italian writing table is a gouache by American artist Willan de Looper (opposite).

ENGLISH COUNTRY UPDATED

nglish country style" is often interpreted as a bower of floral prints. It's a look that can easily be overdone, even for aficionados. So when designer Mark Epstein was called upon to furnish a new Connecticut house using fabrics and upholstered pieces from Laura Ashley, a retailer whose name is practically synonymous with English country, his basic inclination toward simplicity provided welcome ballast for any potential floral excess.

With his associate William McGinn, Epstein created a bedroom that is comfortable and visually rich, yet free of superfluous detail. The expansive windows are partly sheathed in gauze instead of the more elaborate window treatment one might expect to find in such a room. Upholstery fabric was limited to just one floral pattern, and unpretentious sisal matting covers the floor.

The designer's adroit balancing act is evident in the contrast between the creamy monotone color scheme of the walls and floors, and liberal dashes of bright red in the bedskirt and on an upholstered ottoman. The open floor plan is loose and informal, a layout that also prevents the floral fabric from overwhelming the room. Casual country furniture ~ a stripped pine table used as a vanity, a Louis Philippe armoire typical of Provençal farmhouses ~ keeps the feeling light.

An expanse of small-paned windows, the room's outstanding architectural feature, was left mostly bare so as not to compete with the decor. A linen floral print was chosen for the English-style upholstered pieces. Texture is more important than pattern in the scheme of things: Rough sisal on the floor, a shiny red ottoman, and balloon shades of white gauze catch and hold the eye.

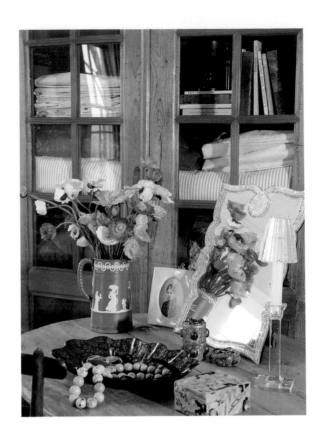

The notion of opposites playing off each other is evident even in this tabletop display (near right): A cleanly stripped pine table is used as an offbeat dressing table, with a glittery Venetian glass mirror, a neoclassical vase, and a bright red papier-mâché bowl. The French armoire behind it holds bed linens and books. An elegant hand-painted screen and silver breakfast service pair gracefully with a provincial antique "yo-yo" coverlet (below right). Against a buttery-cream background, the floral upholstery on an inviting loveseat and chair incorporates all the colors used throughout the room (far right).

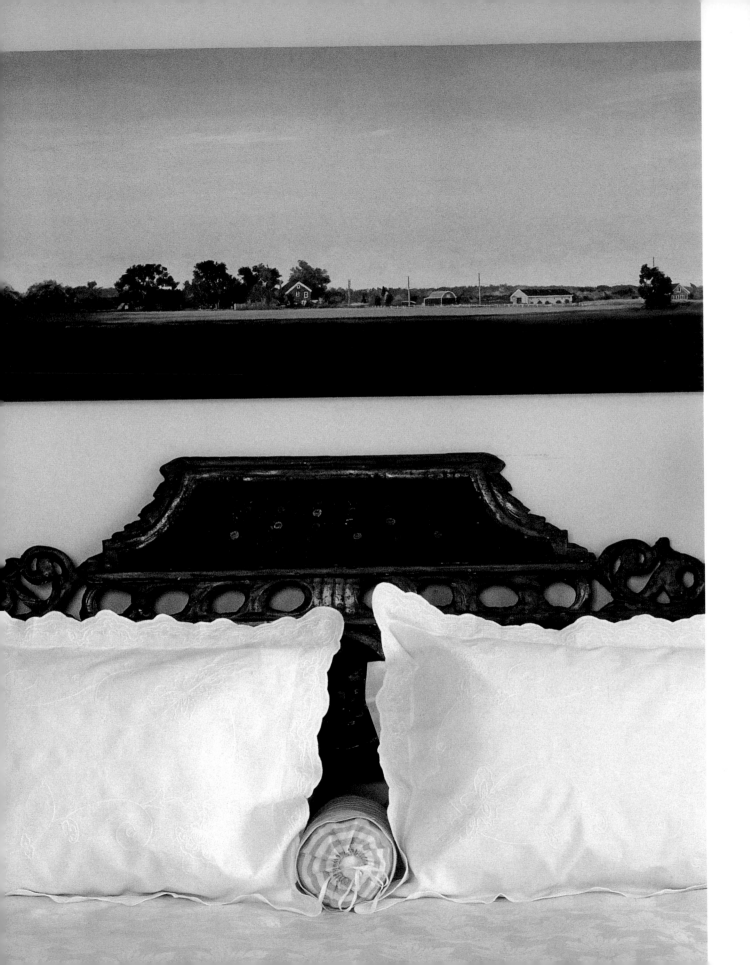

POINT AND COUNTERPOINT

I f an interior designer is like a symphony conductor, orchestrating harmonious agreement between disparate elements, then New York designer Mariette Himes Gomez is something of a maestro. Her trademark approach is a soothing envelope of pale color spiced with strong accents, including occasional doses of bright color, furnishings that make an architectural statement, and idiosyncratic accessories.

In her own Manhattan apartment, Gomez began with vanilla-colored walls, moldings, ceilings, and softly carpeted floor. This created a unifying backdrop for furnishings of different styles and periods, and had the additional advantage of making the apartment's two bedrooms each seem larger, as well as of a single harmonious piece. These two sophisticated rooms are so similar in their feeling of tranquility that they are almost extensions of one another.

Gomez disproves the old saw that small rooms must settle for scaled-down furniture. She chose large, important pieces, such as an eighteenth-century gilt and gesso Spanish headboard (gesso is a plasterlike substance used to prepare a surface for gilding or painting) and a circa 1850 Regency clothespress (essentially an armoire but with drawers at its base)

The sheltering sky of a landscape painting by contemporary artist Ben Schonzeit casts its tranquil vision over Mariette Himes Gomez' bedroom. Its lightness and calmness balance, in a quirky way, the imposing presence of the antique Spanish bed, with its ornate gilt and painted headboard.

for her own room, as well as a fanciful brass bedstead for her daughter's. And she manages to make it all work because there is little else besides the essentials in these two rooms. "Bedrooms are retreats," says Gomez. "I don't think closets and dressing tables should be part of places where one rests."

Touches of color ~ a piece of vintage chintz on an armchair in the designer's bedroom, a raspberry red chair and paisley throw at the foot of her daughter's elaborately curlicued brass bed ~ enliven the creamy palette here and there. Fine antique linens dress both beds, adding a special note of luxury and femininity. "I don't like anything too new," says the designer.

A perfect example of Gomez' sometimes quirky orchestration is the juxtaposition, in her bedroom, of a modern landscape painting above the elaborately carved bed. The painting is a worthy counterpart to the formidable bed in the strength of its imagery and in its equivalent width. The two pieces have no apparent thematic connection, but it is in their very difference that interest and harmony lie. "Together they create style," says Gomez. "It would be pretty boring to put a Madonna above that bed."

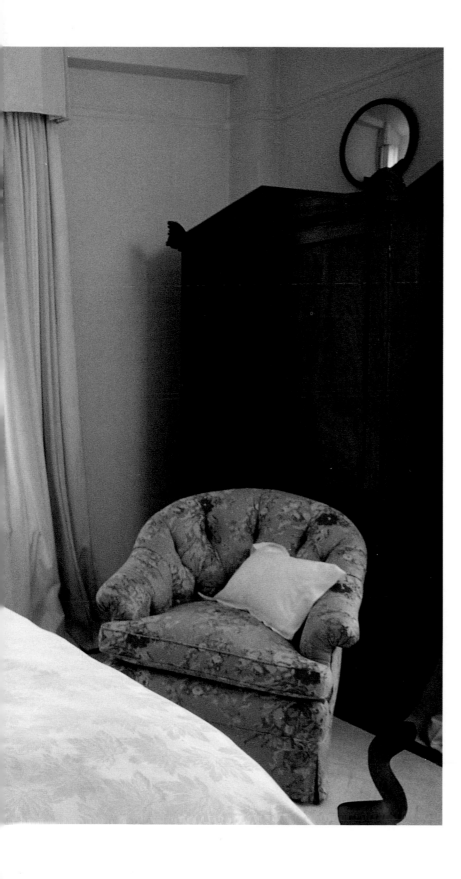

Billowing lace under-curtains provide a light counterpoint to the master bedroom's two massive pieces of furniture: the bed and an English Regency clothespress, which stands tall at its foot. The bed wears a leaf-patterned damask duvet cover; the graceful chair is upholstered in exuberant vintage chintz.

Gomez furnished her
daughter's bedroom with
a nineteenth-century
embossed brass bed
bought in Peru (above
and right). A raspberry-
red-upholstered chair
and red wool paisley bed
throw boldly offset
the predominantly white
color scheme. Light
reflected off the mirror
at the foot of the bed
and through the diaph-
anous bed hangings
imparts a feminine,
ethereal quality.

CHAPTER 3

Personal Taste

y their very private nature, bedrooms offer an opportunity to express personal style to its utmost. They are the perfect setting for a display of unabashed sentiment or idiosyncratic whimsy. All of us experience a sense of extra freedom and pleasure in decorating the bedroom. Less restricted by practicality than other rooms (the kitchen, certainly, or rooms where the television or computer dominates), we are obliged only to our own taste and comfort.

Comfort is key in the bedroom, and that comfort has a psychological dimension as well as a physical one. The bedroom is a place where our interior universe ~ the worlds of memory and fantasy ~ can come into play in subtle and mysterious ways. In the bedroom, favorite pictures, books, heirlooms, and items of sentimental significance contribute to comfort as much as do soft linens and pillows.

Thankfully, no one look dominates our era, as it did in times past. All the old "rules" have gone by the boards, and here, at the turn of the millennium, there is more room than ever in the bedroom for an individual point of view.

SCENE-STEALING STYLE

A muslin-tented bedroom with a polka-dot floor is not, perhaps, for everyone, but to Maine antiques dealer Corey Daniels, "theatrical" is synonymous with personal style. The room is one of fifteen in Daniels' eighteenth-century farmhouse, all furnished with pieces he had stashed away over the years, never knowing exactly where he would use them. Eventually they all found places in the house, whose decor may change radically from one season to the next.

He gave the freest rein to his creative impulses in this bedroom. "It started out as a joke, really," Daniels says of the exotic but inviting chamber, which recalls a Napoleonic-era campaign officer's tent. "It's more 'me' than any other room in the house." The quasi-military theme began as an effort to temper the raw, exposed beams of the peaked ceiling and to cover, quickly and cheaply, unattractively painted wainscoting on the walls. Daniels' first proposed solution was to cut up an old canvas tent; failing that, he bought 100-yard rolls of muslin (for less than one dollar a yard) and began draping. The repeating border of heraldic trim that rings the room at the ceiling was cut from corrugated cardboard; it was born as a tongue-in-cheek allusion to tent flaps, as well as an attempt to cover the drapery tacks that held the muslin in place. As an impulsive final touch, Daniels decided to introduce pattern on the putty-colored wood floor by painting a loose design of white polka-dots.

A definitively masculine atmosphere prevails from the furniture to the accents: a brass campaign bed of the mid-nineteenth century, a heavy vintage trunk at its foot, the weighty terra-cotta jars from Crete, and an American pier table, all part of a subtle, muted palette of browns and golds.

A brass campaign bed, a sturdy spool-turned Victorian armchair, and an Anglo-Indian ebony chair emphasize the very masculine mood of Corey Daniels' tentlike bedroom. An American marble-topped pier table with columns serves as a miniature stage for an ever-changing array of objects, at present a vase with a painted profile and a serious-looking set of leather-bound books.

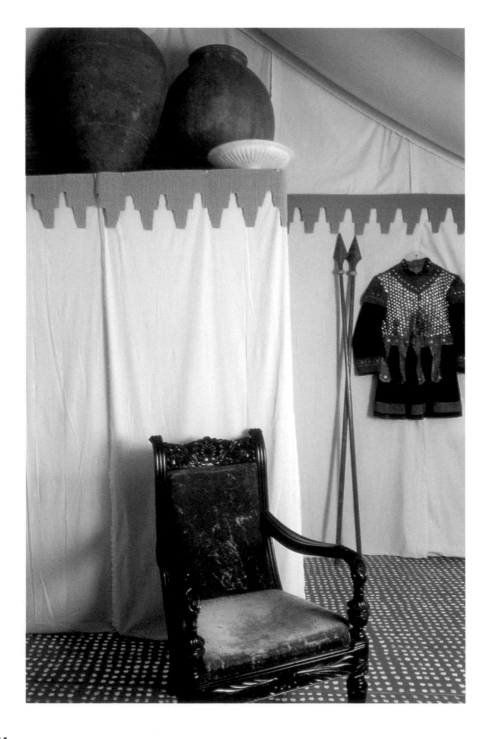

A pair of crossed spears
and a costume jacket
from a Shakespearean
play hanging against
the muslin drapery form
a studied still life (left).
The pieces make wry
reference to theater and
military campaigns,
both of which inspired
the room's decor. Gigantic
terra-cotta jars occupy
an unlikely perch near
the ceiling.

In contrast with
the meticulously staged
master bedroom, the guest
bedroom (opposite) has
a more tranquil and
generic ambience. Anybody
can be comfortable in this
nearly all-white room.

LAYERS OF MEANING

A bed angled rakishly in the bay window and taffeta curtains of pinkest pink are the first clues that here is a very non-conforming stylist indeed. Collage artist and textile designer Carolyn Quartermaine, who also owns a fabric and furnishings shop on London's fashionable Sloane Street, combines the avant-garde artist's sensibility with the traditionalist's predilection for pedigreed antique furnishings. "My style is a blend of the baroque and the contemporary," says Quartermaine. "I take things from the past and use fabrics and color to bring them up to date."

She approaches decorating the same way. "My environments have a sense of collage, of a buildup of paper, fabric, and furniture," she says. "I love hidden layers, revealed one at a time." In her delightfully glamorous London apartment-cum-workshop, part eighteenth-century French chateau and part present-day atelier, Quartermaine offers a decidedly contemporary take on the so-called feminine bedroom. Her own signature silks dress late-nineteenth-century Italian chairs; scribbled over with antique calligraphy, the fabrics take their inspiration from old French script and Mozart manuscripts. Eclectic flea-market finds and humble objects hobnob with formal antique furniture, which is angled casually against white walls with a modernist spareness that is clearly of this century.

Carolyn Quartermaine's roomful of unabashedly original flourishes includes the artist's hand-painted fabrics on a bench and gilded antique chairs, and a shock of brightest pink taffeta at the window. The nineteenth-century French bed "floats" away from the window into the center of the room.

Constantly changing tableaux grace every horizontal surface in Quartermaine's bedroom. On a marble mantel (above left), five carefully positioned pinecones share space with old glass vases and a powder dish, as well as with one of Quartermaine's collages.

A lucite hat stand and other personal treasures make up a second vignette (above right). Mozart's manuscripts inspired the artwork. Stretched across a bench is another of Quartermaine's hand-painted silks ~ this one featuring cut-out birdlike forms.

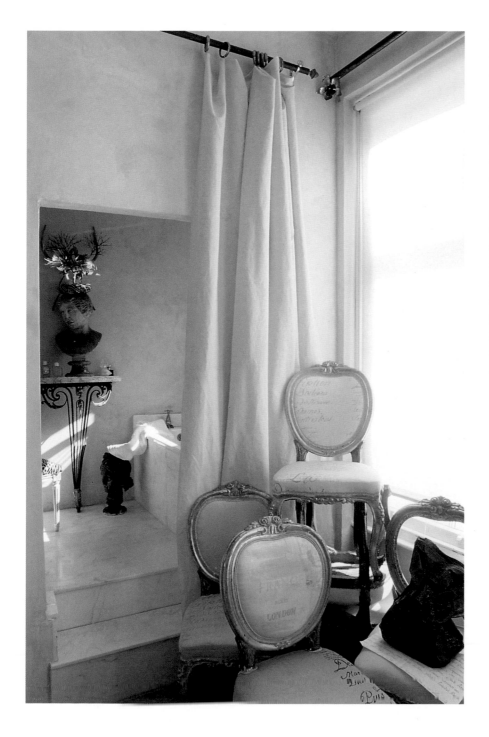

A flotilla of late-nineteenth-century gilded Italian chairs wears Quartermaine's calligraphy-inspired silks. "I like the look of calligraphy, not what it says," the designer explains. "When I make collages out of calligraphy scraps, they take on a language of their own." The "door" between bedroom and bath is a simple, unadorned curtain; a peek into the romantic marble bathroom reveals a plaster copy of a Roman woman's head.

CUTTING-EDGE CRAFTS

Stepping into the Manhattan apartment of Susie Elson, former chairwoman of the American Crafts Council and long-time crafts collector, is like entering a mad, mad world where the very idea of furniture has been wittily, sometimes bizarrely, reinvented. "It's far out of the ordinary," acknowledges Elson, who shares her high-ceilinged duplex with her husband, Edward Elliott Elson, the United States ambassador to Denmark. To achieve this pointedly individualistic decor, Elson commissioned all the furnishings from top artisans in their field.

Like a modern-day Medici, Elson is a patron of the art furniture world, giving craftspeople the freedom to create one-of-a-kind designs. "These are the antiques of the future," she believes. Things made years ago under her farsighted patronage still look very much of the moment. "If something is genuinely exciting," she says, "it will continue to be so." As if to prove the point, all the rooms in the sunlit apartment are filled with wonderful handcrafted oddities ~ including a cubist-inspired grand piano with exaggerated geometric planes and trapezoidal legs and twisted-metal chairs in the shape of human figures. "I like things that have a sense of humor, that are on the cutting edge," she says.

In the master bedroom, the dominating presence is a contemporary interpretation of a historic four-poster bed, the posts punched through with Swiss-cheese-like holes. The guest bedroom, in turn, features a writing table and chair from an avant-garde Japanese workshop; its adjoining sitting room nods to craftsmen of the past with a showcase filled with Greek and Roman antiquities. "A bedroom is a place where one spends a great deal of time," says Elson. "It should have joie de vivre, not be staid or humdrum."

In the guest bedroom, a freewheeling mix of animal-print fabrics dresses the bed. In one corner a Japanese writing table holds a collection of ceramic bowls and framed prints; the chair, also Japanese, is distinguished by a metal sunburst back and a seat of lacquered wood. The sitting room beyond is furnished with a classic piece by Le Corbusier and a postmodern tower cabinet from Germany.

For the master bedroom
(right), Edward Zucca
made a four-poster
bed of bleached maple,
then finished it with silver
leaf and black ebony
detailing. A glass-top
table by Peter Pierborn
has seven unmatching
ebony legs (above).
The aluminum wing-back
angel chair, by Mark
Brazier-Jones, features
a plump upholstered
velvet seat sitting atop
legs with eyeballs.

Surface Appearances

t all begins with the envelope ~ floors, ceilings, walls, and even windows. The surfaces that enclose a bedroom ~ whether a snug guest hideaway tucked under a sloping roof or a sleek and spacious master suite ~ define its proportions and give the space its basic character. From these fundamental relationships a design can evolve. Sometimes one compelling physical attribute can be the starting point for the design that follows. Perhaps the ceilings are rustic wood beams of an old country church, or the walls are made of translucent glass block, or there is an expanse of beautifully aged wood floors.

Often the dictates of location or even climate are so important that choices of materials are narrowed down. Tile makes more sense than carpet in an Arizona bedroom, for example, while windows with a magnificent view require a different approach from those that face a busy street.

Even if the starting point is an unadorned room with walls of simple sheetrock and floors of plain wood, it is an invitation to the designer to address the envelope ~ and perhaps even push it a bit.

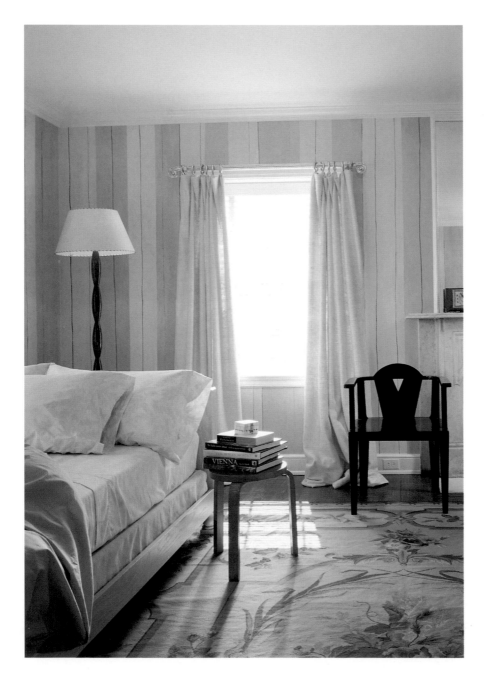

To sound an upbeat note in this spacious bedroom, designer Gary Paul chose an unusual, hand-painted wallpaper ~ a lighthearted takeoff on a conventional buttoned-down stripe. The curtain panels are made of raw silk. A new Chinese needlepoint rug in the Aubusson style was chosen for the way its beige ground and mint green and pink detail tie in with the wallpaper's coloring, and for the way its formal pattern plays against the verticality of the painterly walls.

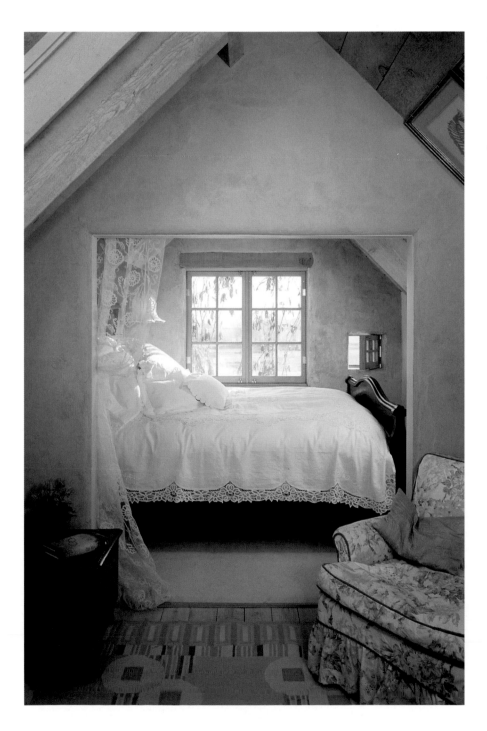

A *tiny bedroom*
tucked under a steep-
pitched roof in this
Colorado house features
rough plaster and old
wooden beams salvaged
from a tumbledown
building nearby. The
room's enormous
character belies the fact
that this is a newly
built retreat. Lacy bed-
clothes provide an
unexpected counterpoint
to all the rusticity.

The restored flower beds outside ~ originally planted by Louise Beebe Wilder, a famous garden writer of the early 1900s ~ inspired the decor of this country bedroom in upstate New York. Designer David Easton installed new French doors so that the room would "reach out to nature." Oak ceiling beams stained to look old remind the owner of summers spent in France. The French terra-cotta tile floor "flows" in from adjoining rooms.

"Bringing the outside in" was a tenet of mid-century modernism; this house, designed by Bauhaus architect Marcel Breuer in the 1950s, is almost an extension of the natural landscape. In one bedroom (opposite), walls of rugged Maryland stone, carefully placed to show off its shape and color, create a powerful abstract composition. The huge glass sliding doors extend the space visually into the woods. In another bedroom (above), a bluestone floor is a cool complement to the woven grasscloth "wainscoting" and nubby wall hangings. The wall-hung desk and credenza echo the low horizontal lines of the house.

CONCRETE REFLECTIONS

Sunlight, and its reflection on water, are prime elements in the decoration of this contemporary Florida home. All the main rooms in the vast, E-shaped house are organized around a 47-foot swimming pool that comes almost to the ground-level windows. Light bounces off the swimming pool through the square-mullioned, floor-to-ceiling windows, penetrating the house even in winter when the sun is at a low angle. It flickers on white walls and floors made of summerstone, a precast concrete paving material that runs through the house and outside into the pool courtyard. "Water is a great architectural tool," says Washington, D.C., architect Hugh Newell Jacobsen. "It was an intentional part of the design."

In a highly practical choice of materials, the designer paved the master bedroom with the same summerstone, a textured snow-white material that has imprints of coral in it. He continued the summerstone right through the bedroom's sybaritic bath, a freestanding little pavilion linked to the bedroom by a corridor. Nonslippery and treated with waterproof sealant, this flooring is ideal for a house where trekking between the pool and the interior goes on all day. It also helps keep the rooms cool. To minimize the need for air-conditioning, every room was designed with two exposures for cross-ventilation and relies on ceiling fans to keep the air moving.

But the main feature of the house remains the light and its reflections. The bedroom walls and ceilings wear a straightforward coat of flat white paint, forming a clean, contemporary canvas on which light and its interplay on water act out their dramatic roles.

Architect Hugh Newell Jacobsen's passion for classical order and symmetry is expressed in the windows in the master bedroom, which run the full 10 feet from floor to ceiling. Jacobsen also designed the four-poster bed, made of steel pipe with faux bronze finish, specifically for the room.

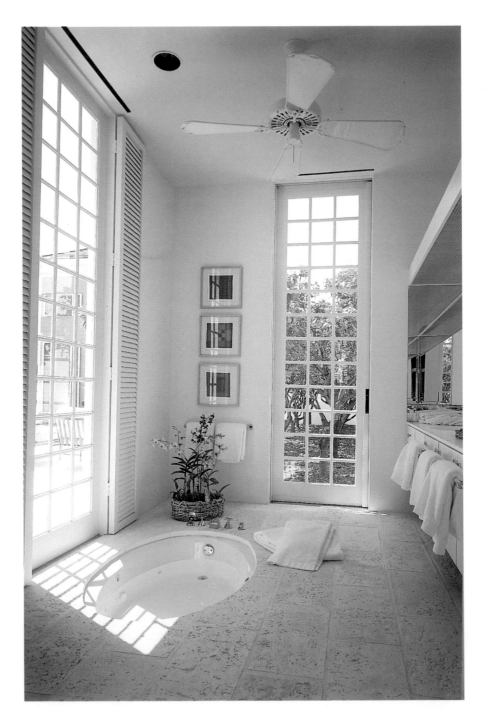

The bath pavilion,
with an oval tub sunk
into white summerstone
flooring, features a
ceiling-high door to the
garden beyond (left). A
grove of grapefruit trees
shields the room from
view, but tall louvered
shutters can be closed
for greater privacy.

The adjoining master
bedroom (opposite),
a classic white box with
unadorned plasterboard
walls and ceiling and
the same summerstone
flooring, might seem anti-
septic in cooler climes;
in subtropical Florida,
its coolness is welcome.

Beds and Beyond

aybed, sleigh bed, or canopy bed ~ a bed is, of course, the one given in a bedroom, and by virtue of its significance as much as its size, it generally occupies center stage. But even given its preeminence, a bed may be imposing or retiring, formal or informal. The traditional four-poster, for example, will immediately assert its sturdy presence in the largest room. But the curtains and lines of the contemporary four-poster can impart a lightness unknown to its medieval forebears.

A simple bed, such as a futon on a platform, will allow other pieces to establish the mood of the room ~ an antique armoire, perhaps, or an inviting armchair. Auxiliary pieces ~ desk, chairs, vanity, nightstand ~ should do more than look pretty. "Everything must be functional," says designer De Bare Saunders. "Even an antique desk should have a useful writing surface, not just be there for decoration."

Freed from the "matched suites" that once enjoyed great popularity, we can forage through history for inspiration. It is only fitting that in this most personal room, furniture is mixed and matched ~ old with new, antiques with reproductions ~ to personalize the space.

Manhattan designer
Debra Blair chose
reproduction furniture
with an exotic Anglo-
Indian look ~ a metal
bed with a tent-shaped
top, left bare except
for sheer batiste drapery
panels, and a cane

and teak "planter's
chaise" ~ for a show-
house bedroom. Indian
rugs over textured
sisal on the floor, glazed
pomegranate-red walls,
and a cerulean-blue ceil-
ing form a rich tableau.

Quirky and colorful,
with red and white
floral-papered walls and
turquoise floors, this
bedroom by Brian
Murphy of the venerable
Parish-Hadley decorat-
ing firm is anchored by
a four-poster bed with
pineapple finials. An
African-American snake
quilt (intended to keep
evil spirits away while
its owner sleeps) and
a 1950s circular hooked
rug with a sea-creature
motif add even more
layers of pattern.

*The elegant curvature
of the iron four-poster
bed echoes this bedroom's
distinctive tentlike ceiling.
Atlanta designer Nancy
Braithwaite chose
reproduction pieces for
this house ~ Regency-style
carved gilt armchairs
and a French Empire-
style cherry center table ~
as counterpoints to the
room's contemporary
architecture. Sunny yellow-
striped walls, sumptuous
bed hangings, and white
silk upholstery on the
sofa convey cheerfulness
and elegance in equal
measure. A yellow and
white linen print borders
the white damask bed
hangings, pillows, and
bedskirt, as well as the
Roman shades.*

This inviting nap spot
and sometime guest room
occupies one end of a
long narrow kitchen in
the Kansas City house of
decorative arts dealers
Bruce Burstert and
Robert Raymond Smith.
They sought out indige-
nous American furniture
~ a Missouri-made wal-
nut daybed more than
150 years old, a slip-
covered chaise, an
American Queen Anne–
style tea table, and a New
England cupboard
still wearing its original
red paint ~ to comple-
ment the house's colonial
design roots.

Pride of place in this cozy bedroom under the eaves of a Martha's Vineyard seaside estate goes to a custom-made copy of a traditional Empire sleigh bed. The commodious curves of its headboard and footboard make it a compelling focal point in the small room.

For decoration, New York design team Tom Fox and Joe Nahem capitalized on the owners' collection of antique fishing lures. A vintage electric fan hums with a nostalgic whirr.

*A quick and clever
solution to the question
of privacy in a guest
room shared by twin beds
is this freestanding, three-
part screen. Painted
to look like button-tufted
upholstery, the screen
separates the beds, at the
same time effectively
carving out a nook for a
dressing table. Simple
wood bedsteads and
a color scheme of pale
blues and creams create
the feeling of a classic
Swedish country interior.*

Designer Glenn Gissler
turned a cozy seaside
bedroom into a sitting
room with an upholstered
twin-size bed (above). A
custom-built oak frame
and piles of pillows fur-
ther disguise the bed. An
Asian storage box cov-

ered with parchment
serves as a coffee table.
  A charmingly sedate
guest bedroom in a rural
New Jersey farmhouse
is furnished with a
French Empire enameled
metal sleigh bed and an
antique English sewing

table used as a night-
stand (opposite). The
idea, says Jorge Letelier,
the architect who owns
this weekend home,
was to evoke the feeling
of a fine old country
house in Brittany.

Headboards can be a
functional backrest
and a decorative focal
point of almost architec-
tural importance.
Here, Mariette Himes
Gomez joined twin-
size mahogany Empire
headboards with
bronze d'oré trim to
make a king-size
bed. A tall nineteenth-
century screen behind
the headboard gives the
bed still greater height.

A *lacy scrollwork head-board* is the outstanding decorative feature in a bedroom where under-statement rules. Like a pen and ink drawing on a blank page, its silhouette is sharp against the room's subtle patterns and textures. On the bed, for example, though everything is white, the matte linen duvet, shams, and bedskirt contrast with the sheen of the pillowcases and top sheet. A *classical medallion* and swag cotton print on an antique chair at the foot of the bed is another decorative flourish.

A fabulous Art Nouveau bentwood bed by the Thonet Brothers furniture makers, found in a Paris flea market, is part of a wide-ranging selection of decorative arts in a Connecticut collector's home (above). The curvaceous loveseat is also a nineteenth-century European bentwood piece. White walls and simple bed dressings allow the strong, sinuous lines to dominate the room.

A distinguished guest bedroom in Jorge Letelier's New Jersey country house features an antique metal bed from Italy, an Empire chair, and a Greek revival urn lamp on a skirted table (opposite). In such refined surroundings, the choice of art on the wall ~ a contemporary painting of suburban houses and mailboxes in lurid colors ~ comes as a bit of a shock. "I find it fresh, friendly, and amusing," says the designer ~ a reminder "not to take things so seriously."

Trim yet glamorous, this bedroom by Los Angeles designer Michael Berman relies on large-scale pieces for impact (left). A sheet-metal sleigh bed with Art Deco curves combines with an imposing fruit-wood armoire (housing an audio-video system), a spirited pair of roll-arm club chairs in bold black and cream stripe, and an oval ottoman with long cord trimming. Celadon green walls form a soothing backdrop. The designer's X-legged writing table and wool-upholstered chair (above), with its voluptuous form and satin-finish legs, take inspiration from such 1940s masters as Jean-Michel Frank and T. H. Robsjohn-Gibbings.

*Genuine antiques mix
unabashedly with
reproductions against the
wood-paneled wall
of a nineteenth-century
farmhouse bedroom
in upstate New York. The
low poster bed ~ simple,
graceful, and strong of
line ~ is newly made, as
are the slipcovered
club chairs and ottoman.
The circular end table
in the foreground
is a contemporary craft
piece. Everything else ~
the faded Oriental rug,
weighty silver candlestick,
vintage velvet throw
pillows, and toile de Jouy
bed covering ~ has
been mellowed and soft-
ened by time.*

There's nothing more gracious or convenient than a separate room reserved for getting dressed. Mariette Himes Gomez took the space seriously, choosing furniture of consequence, including a gleaming Empire dresser and an English chaise longue with a hinged cushion that opens for storage (opposite). Clear panes of glass in all the doors were replaced with mirrors. Beige basketweave carpeting sets the room apart from the adjoining master bedroom, which has bare floors.

Storage pieces need not always be used in the room for which they were intended. In the Newport, Rhode Island, summer house bedroom of the late interior designer Robert Hill, an antique French kitchen hutch has been pressed into service as a bookcase (above). Its distressed white finish helps the piece blend easily with the white-stained oak floors and soft gray-beige walls that form the pale envelope of the room.

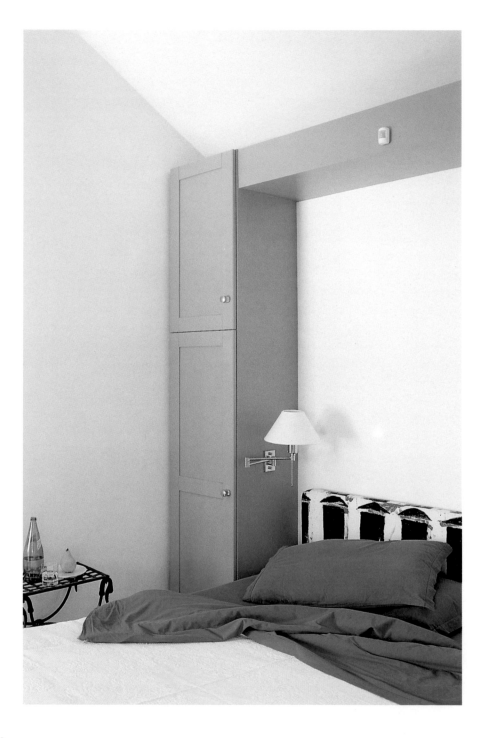

These compact storage cupboards were designed by Milan-based architect Gae Aulenti for a friend's seaside retreat (left). In keeping with a week-end house whose focus is the outdoors, most of the furniture is kept simple and is built-in.

A freestanding storage unit (opposite) is the centerpiece of a commodious dressing room in a new suburban house by architects Shelton, Mindel. Resembling a giant jewelry box, it opens on all four sides, revealing a dressing table within.

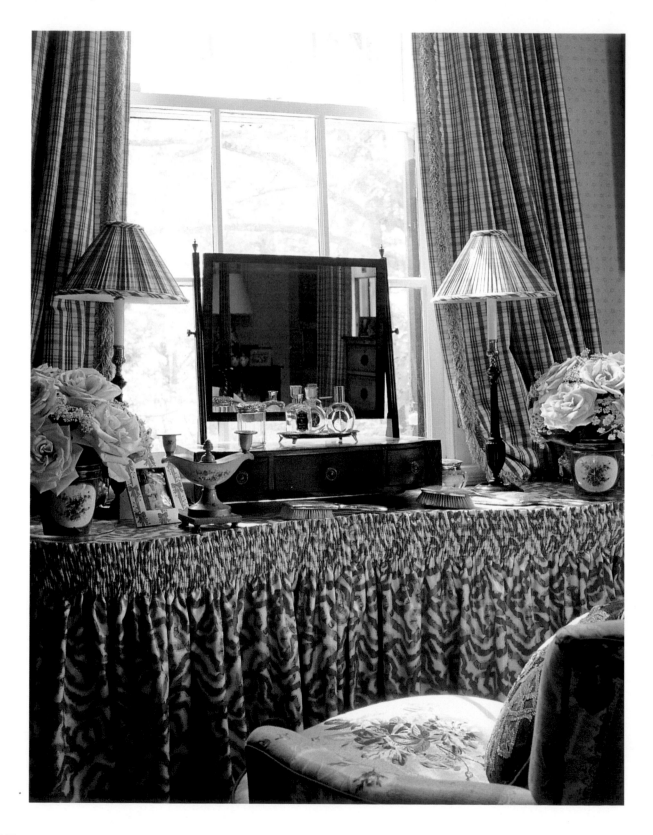

Atlanta decorator
Jane Williamson devised
a charming, feminine
vanity to just fit in front
of a sunny window
(opposite). The serpentine
front was cut from
plywood, then smocked
like a little girl's dress
with red and white
ribbon-patterned fabric.

Long Island designer
Pat Sayers chose historic
lilac-pattern fabric,
topped with a piece of lace
cutwork, to form the
dressing table skirt (right).
Beneath the surface is
a simple, white-painted
plywood box with cubby
holes for storage.

SOLID COMFORTS

*T*here is not a piece of furniture in this urbane bedroom designed for a gentleman that does not have serious presence. Each carefully chosen item stands by itself; some, like a Biedermeier bed and turn-of-the-century Austrian desk, are practically small buildings in their own right.

All of this is, of course, no accident. "The room itself was modern and somewhat lackluster," says designer De Bare Saunders, "so we chose furniture of great architectural interest." The pieces were selected individually, not all purchased at one time. "We put little in, but each piece is in scale with the others and with the architecture of the room," says Saunders. The pediment-topped headboard on that remarkable bed, for example, reminds the designer and his partner, Ronald Mayne, of the Italian Renaissance architect Palladio (in the oval is an exquisite oil painting of Mercury tying his shoe). The substantial armchair is a leather reproduction of a classic Art Deco design. Amid all this solidity of form, the charcoal and ivory zebra-striped rug makes a bold graphic statement of its own, as does the striped wallpaper, whose camel color complements the wood tones of the furniture.

What makes it all work? "Everything's very clean-lined, no matter what period or century," says Saunders. "It was all modern for its day."

There are no "throw-away" pieces in this masculine bedroom created by Ronald Mayne and De Bare Saunders. Everything from the austerely simple Austrian desk to the leather armchair stands on solid, almost sculptural ground.

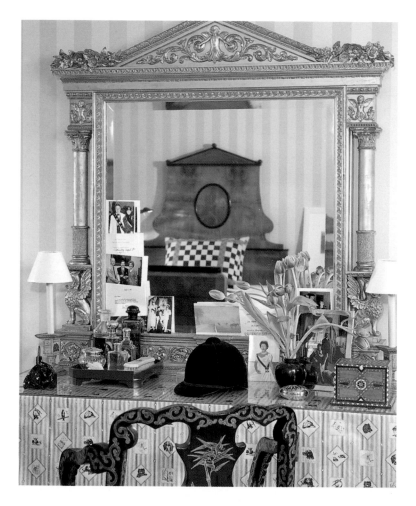

An 1890s gilded
vanity mirror, set within
a Corinthian temple
frame, echoes the
pedimented headboard it
reflects (left). Its richness
is balanced by a tailored
striped chintz on the gentleman's dressing table
and tempered by personal
mementos tucked into
the frame of the mirror.
Painted gold flowers
adorn the backrest of a
Chinese black lacquer
chair. The streamlined
leather armchair offers
an irresistible place
to read (opposite). At the
window, a valance and
cafe curtain of seersucker
trimmed with unfussy
cotton fringe and hung
loosely from curtain
tiebacks allow a soft light
to penetrate the room.

Dressing the Room

The lavish use of fabric in a bedroom still signifies what it did in Louis XIV's France: luxury. The swags, festoons, and tassels of brocade, damask, and silk in a fashionable seventeenth-century boudoir also provided privacy and a certain degree of warmth against the elements. But by the late nineteenth century, interest in the healthful effects of fresh air led to a much lighter, fresher look. Today, anything goes.

Today's fabrics of choice may be gauzy white cottons, ever-popular chintzes (whose lush floral patterns are still based on nineteenth-century favorites), natty stripes, carefree checks, or restful solids, which can be an antidote to the profusion of pattern often found elsewhere in the house.

Fabric-covered furniture ~ headboard, chairs, skirted vanity ~ provide additional opportunities to experiment. Pretty pleats and even contrasting piping can unify several different pieces and lend a layer of eye-catching detail. In recent years, sheets ~ prehemmed, seamless, and in marvelous patterns ~ have made department stores a wonderful resource for decorating the bedroom.

This voluminously draped pine four-poster belonging to designer and writer Alexandra Stoddard is a cocoon from which its occupants can enjoy a fire in the facing hearth. The white hangings fall in a generous floor-length flounce, tamed by the crispness of blue and white striped pillows and a classic American quilt (above).

Pillowcases and sheets patterned with overscaled roses and an heirloom quilt in a classic star pattern make this attic bedroom look soulful and sweet (opposite).

Oceans of fabric in the
colors of sunshine and
ripe fruit ~ mainly
a printed French cotton
combining floral and
paisley motifs ~ elevate
this grandly proportioned
showhouse bedroom to
levels of fantasy reminiscent of England's Royal
Pavilion in Brighton.
The custom canopy, made
of thick swags of fabric
cascading from a conical
crown known as a lit à
la Polonaise, and a V-
shaped window valance
trimmed with tinkly gold
bells are delightfully
fanciful. "I didn't want
anything stodgy or
uptight," says designer
Barbara Ostrom.
Upholstered panels on
the headboard and foot-
board match the fabric
on the bolster and
bedcover, to add an
aura of coziness.

In a room that is
a model of Zen under-
statement, with a
controlled palette of
sandy neutrals, carefully
tailored bed-linens
take center stage (above).
The soft-toned duvet
cover and pillowcases
on the low platform bed
give the room a contem-
porary, tailored look.
Striped edging and but-
tons on the pillows are
handsome details (left).

Demure, fresh fabrics ~
lacy Victorian whites
on the bed, a striped tick-
ing slipcover on a chaise
~ stir memories of
childhood summers in
the master bedroom
of a new Ozark retreat
(opposite). The nostalgic
atmosphere warms
up a sparsely furnished
room, whose few pieces
are contributions from
the owners' relatives
and friends.

There is no shortage of fabric in this serene creation by Boston designer Benn Theodore (opposite). A cushioned upholstered headboard in cream cotton harmonizes with the clipped Swiss batiste bed hangings that dress the four-poster. European linens cover a profusion of pillows.

A matching bench curls up at the foot of the bed.

A Connecticut antiques dealer who loves the plain lines of Shaker furniture created these tidy-as-a-bandbox bed enclosures (above). Fresh and crisp, the draped alcoves provide drama in a Shaker-plain guest room.

The headboards, bed-skirts, and canopy linings of blue plaid are in simple but striking contrast to the expanses of white.

For the master bedroom of his eighteenth-century house, the late designer and trompe l'oeil artist Richard Lowell Neas had the bedspread, headboard, and ornamental canopy hand-quilted in a local village. The bed's scalloped baldequin-shaped headboard has a look of provincial formality. The wall's molding and paneling are actually paint on plaster walls.

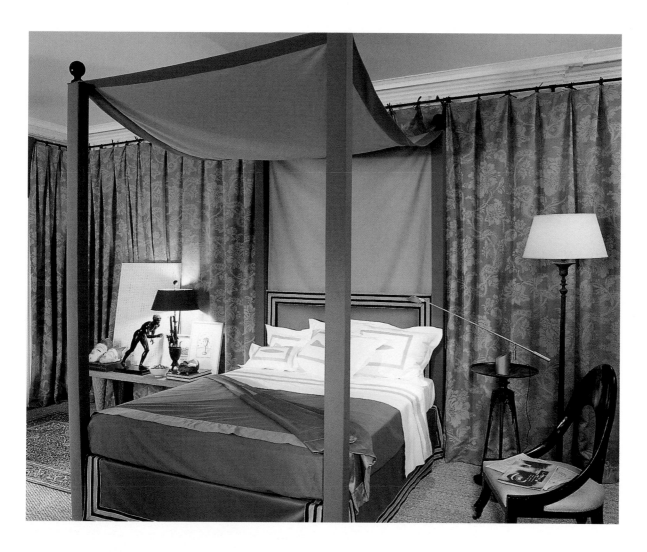

This deceptively casual showhouse bedroom by French designer Yves Taralon ~ a sea of taupe sparked with crisp white linens ~ perfectly illustrates how fabric can be used in a handsome, masculine way. The room's masterstroke: walls draped with sumptuous woven damask that can be easily changed or pushed aside to reach concealed closets; the fabric also provides good insulation against drafts. The bed's simple canopy is of the soft, supple wool flannel more commonly used for men's suiting. Black and white striped grosgrain trim on the headboard and a tailored bedskirt add a heraldic touch.

In this cool, orderly
bedroom, Boston designer
Richard Eustice used
just two fabrics ~ a classic linen stripe in cream
and brown for bed,
windows, windowseat,
and pillows and a white
cotton duck, quilted in
a diamond pattern, for
nonrumpling slipcovers.
The striped fabric was
cut into squares and
reassembled to make a
patchwork bedspread
(right). The window
shades feature pleated
lambrequins.

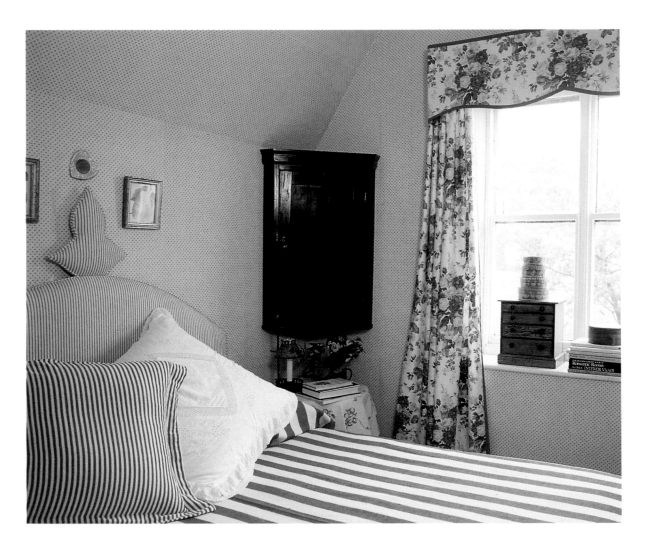

Fabric gives the interior of this Derbyshire gatehouse in England its cheerful demeanor. Sunny yellow enlivens the polka-dot walls and the exuberant floral chintz curtains. A delicate red and white stripe covers the whimsically shaped headboard, while broader and bolder versions of the stripe appear on the bedspread and pillow.

In a small London bed-
room, decorator Lady
Jane Churchill took a cue
from France, where bed-
rooms are often decorated
with just one patterned
fabric. Here a charming
red and white toile de
Jouy upholsters the walls

and headboard and
swaths the windows. A
rosy red braided trim is
used to highlight curtain
details and give the
scheme greater definition.
White lace-trimmed
linens and pillows make
the bed an oasis of calm.

TAILOR-MADE TRANQUILITY

S oothing is the word for this bedroom by designers Charles Spada and Tom Vanderbeck. The color gray, which is often underrated and surprisingly versatile, is the key to this pleasant effect. "I love gray in bedrooms because it's soft, ethereal, and calming," says Spada.

To make the room look all of a piece despite its collection of antique furnishings from disparate sources, the designers used a palette of grays and limited the number of fabrics to just a few unfussy ones. "Forget about heavy lace, chintzes, and brocades," says Spada. "Keep a bedroom minimal, so it's not overbearing. In a bedroom you want to feel calm, not be distracted by a mishmash of things."

For the curtains, tailored bedskirt, headboard, and chaise longue, Spada and Vanderbeck chose a cotton-linen blend, a material they find more practical than linen, which tends to rumple. The custom-made draperies feature inverted pleats, rather than the more traditional pinch pleats, to achieve a richer, fuller, more refined look. A pair of late-nineteenth-century painted French chairs are covered in linen; a little gold footstool is upholstered in gray silk taffeta. Touches of white ~ a strip of edging along the bottom of the bedskirt, simple bed linens ~ provide a refreshing contrast.

Not a ruche or a ruffle finds its way into this smart, tailored bedroom. The headboard is upholstered in a soft gray cotton-linen blend; the bedskirt is of the same fabric edged in white. "Bedrooms shouldn't be overfrilly and suffocating," believes designer Charles Spada. "You can come into this room, take a deep breath, and forget the world."

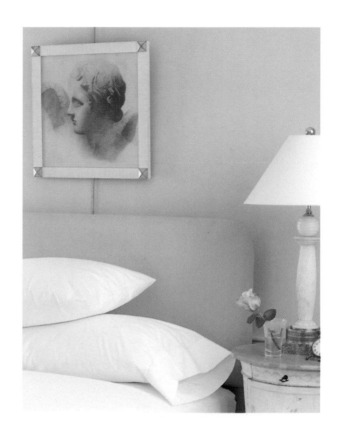

Consistency of color in fabric and paint unifies an assortment of antique European pieces (left). An eighteenth-century French chaise, still bearing its original paint, and the headboard (above) have been upholstered in a durable cotton-linen blend. The demilune commode has a coat of distressed paint that matches the gray fabric.

Final Touches

or many of us when it comes to accessorizing a bedroom, minimalism is not a very appealing concept. Sentimental souvennirs should find a natural home here ~ a pair of antique candlesticks, a vintage radio, some seashells from a vacation, beloved family photographs, favorite books. Together they contribute to the sense of well-being that is the essence of every successful bedroom.

Unlike large pieces of furniture, accents ~ small collectibles, pillows, artwork, for example ~ are easy to vary. Since we spend a lot of time in the bedroom it is important to head off visual ennui. One antiques dealer suggests removing all small objects from time to time and creating new vignettes by bringing pieces out of storage or borrowing them from other rooms. Careful placement and well-conceived displays can make even the most ordinary accessories seem special. "Every object needs a home," says New York designer Mariette Himes Gomez. "When your possessions don't have a home in your bedroom, they're simply clutter. When they're well organized, they become collections."

The repetition of a single simple shape produces a striking wall display in this bedroom by decorator Jeff Lincoln. With little else to distract the eye, the two tiers of six framed antique engravings, viewed through the lines of an undraped iron four-poster, create a harmonious geometry. A pair of white plaster table lamps on either side of the bed, reproductions of a classic Giacometti disc design of the 1940s, underscores the room's decisive symmetry. A carved wooden pineapple, once a finial on the roof of an old building, was chosen for its sculptural quality and hefty scale.

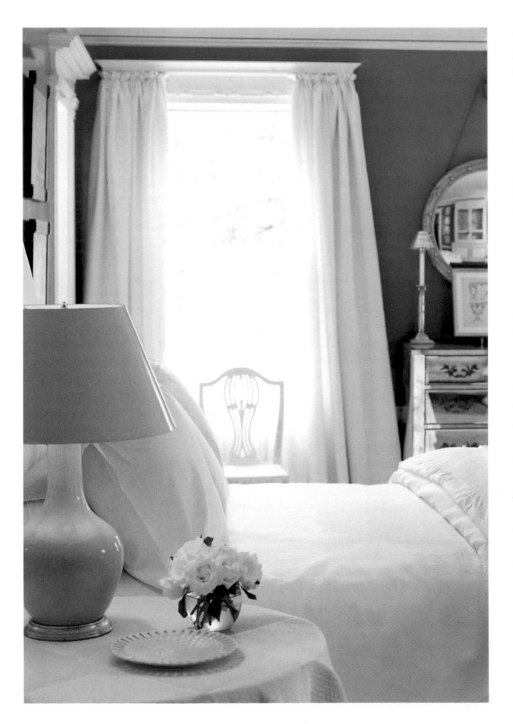

Sparkling accessories play off an intense backdrop of sage-green walls in a crisply elegant bedroom by designers Lee Bierly and Christopher Drake (left). Against this color a gilt-framed bull's-eye mirror stands out. Beneath, an antique mirrored chest is home to a framed drawing on an easel and a pair of candlestick lamps.

Glints of gold and hints of grandeur reminiscent of the Old South are artfully combined in a Louisiana bedroom by designers Ann Holden and Ann Dupuy (opposite). The gold beaded lampshade and gilt sunburst mirror frames add iridescent detail. The cherub hanging from the wrought-iron bed frame adds an unexpected note of whimsy.

A purist ethic, very much in keeping with the traditional Japanese approach to choosing and positioning objects, is at work in this Manhattan high-rise bedroom belonging to design consultant Robert Homma. A century-old statue of Buddha sits atop a lacquered table (opposite). The screen, a contemporary piece made of handmade paper, was picked up at a department store sale. A trio of boldly patterned shells creates a strong still life on a patterned bench. Green vases by a Japanese ceramicist are arrayed on a nineteenth-century scholar's bench traditionally used for calligraphy (above). A contemporary red and gold Japanese lacquer box is used for photo storage, while Shunga prints and woodcuts are propped casually against the wall.

*Even books become
decorative accessories
when displayed in
a glass-fronted Empire
bookcase with old-
world charm (opposite).
The all-white pottery
on the cabinet is one of
several collections
grouped by color in the
Victorian farmhouse
of designer Jorge Letelier.*

    *An ever-changing
array of objects and art-
work marks the
decorating style of
antiques dealer Corey
Daniels (right). This
studied bedside arrange-
ment is composed of
vintage treasures: twin
mercury glass vases, old
framed photographs, and
an alabaster decanter.*

HOMESPUN TRADITION

A love for all things old and handcrafted informs the decor of two bedrooms in the studio of Bob Timberlake, a painter of the American Realist school who also is something of a cultural historian. Timberlake oversees the production of a line of furniture and accessories that captures and preserves the Arts and Crafts heritage of North Carolina, his home state.

To complement native folk furnishings found in the area ~ pie safes with hand-punched tin panels, painted chests, and twig rockers, for example ~ Timberlake collects and reproduces homespun accessories. Among them are quilts, coverlets, pottery (including agateware pitchers), birdhouses, and decoys. All are locally made in the manner of master craftspeople of the past. Pottery bowls are hand thrown and decorated with simple red, blue, and brown glazes typical of the region. Rag rugs are woven on looms just as they were a century ago. Wooden furniture such as beds and chairs are finished to show off the distinctive grains of native cherry and walnut.

Above all, Timberlake appreciates "the way things were made with such love and affection back in the old days," with an innate love of materials ~ the woods, the homespun, the clay ~ that were transformed into furniture, quilts, and pots to be cherished.

The rough-hewn beams and small window of a restored 1807 log home form an authentic setting for reproduction furnishings and accessories with roots in rural North Carolina crafts traditions. In the master bedroom, a chest is hand-painted with Pennsylvania Dutch motifs, and a new quilt reproduces the vivid log cabin pattern. A collection of beautifully framed silhouettes punctuates the geometry of the log-chinking walls.

Vintage toys recalling
a country childhood ~
birchbark canoes on
the wall, a red metal truck
on a sidetable ~ acces-
sorize a guest bedroom in
Bob Timberlake's studio.
A wall shelf above the easy
chair holds a handful
of miniatures. A rag rug,
camp blankets, and boldly
striped bed covers bring
high color to the rustic
decor. Worn blue paint on
a reproduction cabinet
convincingly simulates age.

Photography Credits

1	Christopher Simon Sykes	66	James Yochum	109	Kari Haavisto	
2	Michael Dunne	67	Laurie E. Dickson	110-111	Jeff McNamara	
4	Kari Haavisto	68-69	John Vaughan	112	Esto/Scott Frances (top and bottom)	
7	J. Merrell	70-71	Walter Smalling	113	Richard Felber	
8	Peter Margonelli	72	Robert Lautman	114	Eric Roth	
11	Lizzie Himmel	74-75	Robert Lautman	115	David Phelps	
12	Kari Haavisto	76	Jack Winston	116	Jacques Dirand	
15	Scott Frances	78	Jeff McNamara	117	Walter Smalling	
16	Jeff McNamara	79	Jeff McNamara	118-119	Jeff McNamara	
18	Richard Felber	80-81	Langdon Clay	120	Simon Wheeler	
20-21	Richard Felber	82	Peter Margonelli	121	Christopher Simon Sykes	
22	Antoine Bootz	83	Lizzie Himmel	122	Jeff McNamara	
24-25	Antoine Bootz	84-85	Scott Frances	124-125	Jeff McNamara	
26	Lizzie Himmel	86	Andrew Bordwin	126	Antoine Bootz	
28-29	Lizzie Himmel	87	Jeff McNamara	128-129	Peter Margonelli	
30	Antoine Bootz	88	Antoine Bootz	130	Eric Roth	
32-33	Antoine Bootz	89	William Waldron	131	Lizzie Himmel	
34	Tom Yee	90	Catherine Leuthold	132-133	Antoine Bootz	
36-39	Gordon Beall	91	Jeff McNamara	134	Jeff McNamara	
40	Antoine Bootz	92-93	Grey Crawford	135	Thibault Jeanson	
42-43	Antoine Bootz	94-95	Kari Haavisto	136	Langdon Clay	
44	Thibault Jeanson	96	Antoine Bootz	138-139	Langdon Clay	
46-49	Thibault Jeanson	97	Thibault Jeanson	142	Thibault Jeanson	
50	Antoine Bootz	98	Antoine Bootz			
52	Thibault Jeanson	99	Langdon Clay			
54-55	Thibault Jeanson	100	Walter Smalling			
56	Jacques Dirand	101	Jeff McNamara			
58-60	Jacques Dirand	102	Kit Latham			
62-63	Jacques Dirand	104-105	Kit Latham			
64	Christopher Irion	106	Kari Haavisto			
		108	Elizabeth Zeschin			

Acknowledgments

House Beautiful would like to thank the following homeowners: Jeffrey and Sharon Casdin, Lynn and Kurt Kircher, Pat Guthman, David and Katrin Cargill, Dolph Leuthold, Suzanne and Elliott West.

The photograph on page 16 was taken at the Mansions and Millionaires Showhouse, Sands Point, New York; page 34, the Boston Design Center, Boston, Massachusetts; page 66, the Park Ridge Youth Campus Showhouse, Wilmette, Illinois; page 78, the Mansions in May Showhouse, Morristown, New Jersey; pages 79 and 86, the Southampton Showhouse, Southampton, New York; page 88, the Royal Oak Foundation Showhouse, New York, New York; pages 92 and 93, the Pasadena Showhouse, Pasadena, California; page 96, the Royal Oak Foundation Showhouse, New York, New York; page 100, the Atlanta Symphony Associates Decorators Showhouse, Atlanta, Georgia; page 101, the Mansions and Millionaires Showhouse, Sands Point, New York; pages 102-105, the Litchfield County Designer Showhouse, Roxbury, Connecticut; pages 110-111, the Mansions in May Showhouse, Morristown, New Jersey; page 117, the French Designers Showhouse, New York, New York; pages 118-119, the Junior League of Boston Decorators' Showhouse, Boston, Massachusetts; pages 122-125, the Junior League of Hartford Showhouse, Hartford, Connecticut; pages 128-29, the Locust Valley Showhouse, Locust Valley, New York; page 130, the Junior League of Boston 25th Anniversary Decorator Show House, Boston, Massachusetts.